ent senses, it boasts the longest entry in the dictionary. Some are typeset
you are in difficulty, experiencing a set-back. In the game of bowls a set
udge then you have a se... come to a
riting. A dog pointing its... a good set.
urrent or the wind is its... ow you the
th has fifty threads per in... oth. Tartan
dress or sail hangs, the se... an arm, leg
ge hair while it is still damp so that it is set in a style when it dries. The
sitioned so that they are in opposite directions at precisely the right set
xact positioning of the characters so that they have the right amount of
aised is called its set. In woodwork, the set of the plane can be adjusted.
et is a portion of land marked out for mining. An ornate brooch is set on
o that has been cut up ready for planting is also called a set. Flowers that
y staked is the set. A set in tennis is a group of games. To be at set point
nany pleats, and each one of these pleats is called a set. In film and in the
lar stone used in paving is a set. The last coat of plaster on a wall before
d the object that you are striking. The arrangement of hooks on a fishing
n mining, that is struck with a hammer to cause a crack in the rock face,
c ability are sorted into sets. The Bloomsbury Set was a group of artists,
e and were famous for their unconventional lifestyles and attitudes. The
nat are needed to perform a square dance. A set of tools for a particular
raver's set of prints. A full set of teeth. A handsome face has a good set
A complete collection is a set. Cups and saucers make up a tea set. If you
estate or campus. The set of timbers is a term in mining for a supporting
of sets. If you set something down you are placing it in position. A hen is
to get up again. To sit down for a meal, for example, to set for breakfast.
pefore you. To set foot outdoors. A violent attack is the setting of your
on edge. To set in motion. To set free. To put singers in tune is to set
. To set in hand means to control someone's behaviour. Feet can be set
nething your heart may be set on it. To set eyes on someone means to
A soldier posted in a specific place to set watch is appointed to perform
of harming them. Limits are set so that we have boundaries. Dates can
rk set by their teachers. To start a psalm for others to sing along to is
I that you wish the others to follow. To set things right. A trap can be
in precious metals. False teeth are set on their plates. Setting sail means
ttle. To set the table is to put cutlery and crockery ready for a meal.

I have a spell cheque function
It came with my PC
It plainly marques for my revue
Mistakes I cannot sea.

I strike a key and type a word
And weight for it two say
Weather I am wrong or write
It shows me strait away.

As soon as a mistake is maid
It nose before two long
And I can put the error rite
Its never, ever wrong.

I have run this poem threw it
I am shore you're pleased to no
It's letter perfect to the end
My spell cheque told me sew.

Anonymous

Words Fail Me
Teresa Monachino

For *Anna* Monachino

Foreword

The genesis of this book lies with my mother and her uncertain grasp of English over the years. In my attempts to explain the often extreme differences in meaning between similar-looking words I often found myself equally befuddled. English hoodwinks us into believing one thing while concealing something quite different. All is not what it seems. This book is my attempt to bring these illogical ideas to the fore, not as an academic study of our language but as a visual treat. The typographer and artist Eric Gill didn't learn to read until he was eight, expressing boredom in the presence of something devoid of rhyme or reason. It seemed only fitting therefore to use his typefaces Gill Sans and Joanna to express that irrationality within these pages.

Teresa Monachino

Contradictionary

This section deals with words that are totally insincere and lack any integrity. It points the finger at words that do not mean what they say; words that appear plural but are in fact singular; single letters that have many inconsistent pronunciations; and spellings that are just plain cruel. Where I accuse these words of hypocrisy I have done so in red ink.

Why is abbreviation
such a long word?

Why does monosyllabic
have five syllables?

edalian

means the overuse of long words

lithp

fonetic

a word whose letters

palindrome

emordnilap

read the same in reverse

noses run

feet smell

VERB
is a
NOUN

BELIEVE

quite a lot is a large amount

quite a few is a large amount

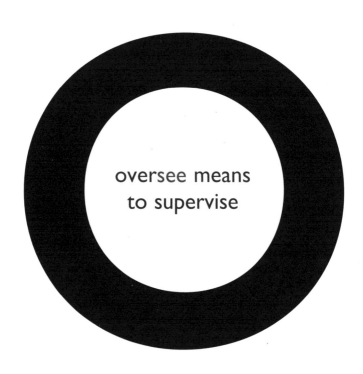

oversee means
to supervise

overlook means
to neglect

Why is it that a man
has more hair than a
his head?

with hair on his head
man with hairs on

To say someone is a vision is to pay them a great compliment. If you say that they look a sight it is a grave insult.

Being blunt can result in a cutting remark

While there are many cases where a double negative conveys a positive, there is no case where a double positive conveys a negative.

yeah, right

This word contains no fewer than four pronunciations of the letter e including one which is silent

re-en

tered

tuff
coff   doe
                boruh
            throo
            thort
        hiccups

Finding a decent home can be really quite tough. You'll find that you may have to cough up a large amount of dough to live in a London borough. Before you start looking through details give it considerable thought so as to avoid any nasty hiccoughs along the way.

Antigrams

Whereas anagrams simply transpose the letters in a word to give us a new meaning, antigrams have a more sinister tendency. Rearranging the letters of the words on the left-hand page gives a new word or phrase on the right that directly opposes or contradicts it. With one shuffle Santa swaps his jolly red cloak for a red-hot number, as he's transformed into a sinister Satan.

astronomers

no more stars

funeral

real fun

honestly

on the sly

within earshot

I won't hear this

medicate

decimate

silent

listen

violence

nice love

forty-five

over fifty

earliest

rise late

commendation

aim to condemn

antagonist

not against

united

untied

elvis

lives

Ambitexterity

A pair of homonyms are two separate words that may be spelt or sound the same but always differ in meaning. Heteronyms, on the other hand, have the same spelling but differ in both pronunciation and meaning. Some examples of both these kinds of verbal oddity are illustrated in the next few pages.

minute

row, row, row,

tear.

wind

wind wind wind wind wind wind wind wind wind wind wind wind wind wind wind wind wind wind wind wind wind wind wind wind wind wind wind wind wind wind wind wind wind wind wind wind wind wind wind wind wind wind wind wind wind wind wind content

(content)

de⌐ect

de ect

?
wonder

DER

BOW

"converse"

converse

close

Pleonasties

This term refers to tautological redundancies: the use of more words than are necessary for the expression of an idea. A pleonasm usually consists of two words, one of which is redundant. Why use two words when one will do? It's ~~mentally~~ insane. In the next few pages the redundant word is shown blushing red.

unexpected surprise

free gift

advance warning

frozen ice

honest truth

stupid idiot

empty space

assemble together

end result

past experience

rough estimate

actual facts

multiple choice

successfully pass

armed gunman

terrible **disaster**

close **proximity**

yell loudly

Antagonyms

This term describes two words spelt the same and
pronounced the same but which directly oppose
each other in meaning, depending on their context.
In the illustrations I have let the words explain for
themselves — it's the very least they can do.

THE LIGHTS ARE
OUT

THE STARS ARE
OUT

screen

screen

(departed)

LEFT

(remaining)

[BUCKLE

BUCKLE

B   UND

clip

clip

Oxycretins

Oxymorons are figures of speech in which contradictory terms appear in conjunction with each other, for instance 'pretty ugly'. I didn't want to include these, however, as I felt they were too obvious. Less obvious perhaps are their single-word versions. Believe it or not the complete opposite can be housed within the same word. These are exposed by removing a single letter, hardly in deep disguise but unnoticed all the same. Simply remove the letter in red to reveal the contradictory word.

charm

seven

whole

prude

slaughter

twit

resign

feast

stray

friend

threat

covert

(sic) Note

Some words are made up of two words that, when separated or hyphenated, bear no resemblance to the original meaning. They have to be very carefully typeset. With one shoddy word break the meaning becomes compromised, often with extremely unfortunate results. I found these particular leg-ends in various newspapers and magazines.

Working with you regularly, either in an individual session or within a group, therapists are available either in hospitals or offices, providing treatment for people of all ages whose functioning is impaired.

An inscribed book is one which has been signed by the author or some other notable person as a memento for the recipient.

Although some persistence is required by the children, their learning through discovery often contributes more effectively to their education.

This internationally renowned, specialist bookstore carries an extensive collection of first editions that you will find nowhere in any store in London.

Finally the bill would go to the House of Lords where we would hope that those titled gentlemen may defeat it.

The ad agency said that they would begin their new campaign.

Acknowledgements

For their invaluable, which means valuable, help I would like to thank Emilia Terragni and Rebecca King at Phaidon, Caspian Dennis at Abner Stein and most of all Alan Fletcher.

Every effort has been made to acknowledge sources quoted in this book. The author will be pleased to incorporate any inadvertent omissions in future editions.

Pages 24-25, reprinted with permission of Atria Books, an imprint of Simon & Schuster Adult Publishing Group, from *Crazy English* by Richard Lederer, Revised Edition. Copyright © 1989, 1990, 1998; pages 28-29, extract from *Word For Word* by Stewart Clark and Graham Pointon, Oxford University Press, 2003.

Phaidon Press Limited
Regent's Wharf
All Saints Street
London N1 9PA

Phaidon Press Inc.
180 Varick Street
New York, NY 10014

www.phaidon.com

First published 2006
© 2006 Phaidon Press Limited

ISBN 0 7148 4635 X

Designed by Teresa Monachino

Printed in China

Sharpening a razor is known as setting its edge. Preparing a scene is se
a musical instrument is to set it. If you set a piece of leather you are st
Butterflies arranged in a case are set. Making a required adjustment to
is punctual. A rate of tax can be set at a certain percentage. To set a ca
you set them before that person. The value or price of something is s
hand, to set little store by something holds it in contempt. A determi
set in an expression. Clenched teeth are teeth that are set. Your mo
that is overloaded and becomes bent or twisted as a result has becom
in hot water until the point of setting then pour the liquid into a mou
a three-coat process: render, float and set. In sheep breeding, the est
accustomed to the bowling he is set. The position taken by dancing par
such as east northeast. To set forth is to begin on a journey. A wind car
them. Emphasising a point is setting it home. A current may set a boat
as a setting pole. To set your face for home is to point it in that direc
To busy yourself is to set about doing something. To set the dogs on s
at each other beak to beak. A person may be set against another in a
upon. To set about a piece of gossip is to spread it around. To set abro
rising to the surface are set in motion. Your head can be set afloat wh
is setting it apart. Putting an object away until it is required is setting it
can be set aside for a particular purpose. A set-back hinders progress.
To set by for future use. Slackening the pegs of a musical instrument
shape. To place an object on the ground is to set it down. A taxi se
doing something is to be devoted to a task. A proclamation may be se
grievances is an invitation to express them in words. A person can b
when it is gathered. An alarm is set off when it rings. A spark could se
be set off against each other to form a contrast. Flattering clothing ca
gain in another area in order to balance the books. In printing, setting
To set out your throat is to cry out loud. Market stalls set out their g
Doing what you set out to do is the accomplishment of a predeterm
them. To set a person over is to have them killed. To set to one's ha
racing to get to the front is an attempt to set-to. A set-up is a contri
or flag hoists it up. To set up your bristles means to become irate. To
used for putting drinks down on the bar ready for consumption. It'
handle a particular task. A taxidermist mounting an animal in a life-like
grow up and leave home to set up a new life for themselves. If you se
that they need. Set places are positions that have been designated. A